RESPONDING
TO
LITERATURE
WRITING AND THINKING ACTIVITIES
GRADES 1-3

Sandra M. Simons, Ph.D.

Anne P. Maley

Sandra Forrest
Illustrator

Alicia Martinez, Ed.D.
Bilingual Education Consultant

Jane Morris, Ph.D.
Whole Language Consultant

EUGENE, OREGON

ISBN 0-9627689-2-8

CONTENTS

RECORD-KEEPING CHARTS

TO THE TEACHER

Responding to Literature: Writing and Thinking Activities is a teaching aid for use in your reading or language arts classroom. It contains 58 reproducible generic reading **Response Activities** that may be used with any reading selection and 8 reproducible **Record-Keeping Charts** to assist you in monitoring and managing students' reading. The **Response Activities** may be used in a variety of ways to adapt to your reading curriculum and teaching style as well as to the abilities and learning styles of your students.

INSTRUCTIONAL FEATURES

Response Activities enhance your reading instruction by:

- integrating reading, writing, and thinking

- providing open-ended assignments that encourage students to express their own reactions to and opinions about what they read

- requiring students to think critically about what they have read

- encouraging creative responses that extend thinking beyond the reading selection

- motivating students to derive personal meaning from their reading

Response Activities help you meet the needs of all students by:

- providing a variety of activities to accommodate students with different learning styles and varying abilities

- providing open-ended activities to challenge talented and gifted students

- providing nonthreatening, motivating activities that at-risk students can and will do

- providing opportunities for ESL students to participate in class with personal responses to what they read

ORGANIZATIONAL FEATURES

Record-Keeping Charts help you monitor students' reading by:

- providing a variety of simple formats that students can use to record what they read

- encouraging students to take responsibility for keeping track of their own reading

Response Activities supplement any reading program. Use them with:

- **whole language and literature-based reading programs**

    The response activities are generic and may be used with any literature selection.

    Assign response activities to individuals, to a small group of students reading the same book, or to the entire class. If the entire class reads the same book, you may have all students complete the same activity or assign activities based on each student's need, ability, and learning style.

    Augment your instruction by using response activities that focus on literary elements or genre. For example, if you are teaching characterization, you may assign one of the nineteen response activities that focuses on character.

- **independent reading programs**

    The generic nature of the activities makes them applicable to any book students choose.

    The variety of activities enables you to make assignments that are appropriate for each student's ability and learning style.

    The response activity format is easy for students to complete independently.

- **basal reading programs**

    Use response activities with stories in your basal reading program.

Response activities accommodate your teaching style. Use them with:

- **cooperative group instruction**

    The response activities may be used as a basis for small group assignments and discussions.

- **whole-class instruction**

- **individualized instruction**

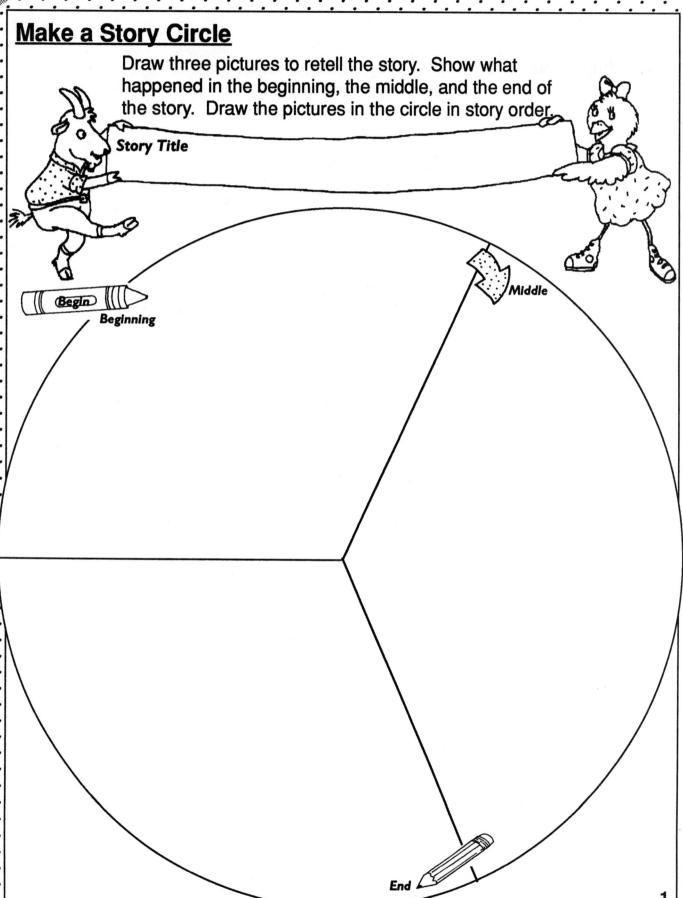

Make a Story Circle

Draw three pictures to retell the story. Show what happened in the beginning, the middle, and the end of the story. Draw the pictures in the circle in story order.

Story Title

Begin

Beginning

Middle

End

Complete a story circle

Reading Focus

plot - beginning, middle, end
plot - main events

Teaching Suggestions

Review the concepts of the beginning, middle, and end of a story. Use examples from familiar stories to illustrate the concepts.

Oral Language Activities

Have students use their story circles to retell the story to a small group.

ESL students: Allow students to retell the story in their native language. Pair limited English proficiency students with English dominant students who will act as translators for the class.

Extension Activity

Writing
Have students use the events in their story circle to write a story summary.

Name

What's the Problem?

Fill in the story map to tell what happened in the story.

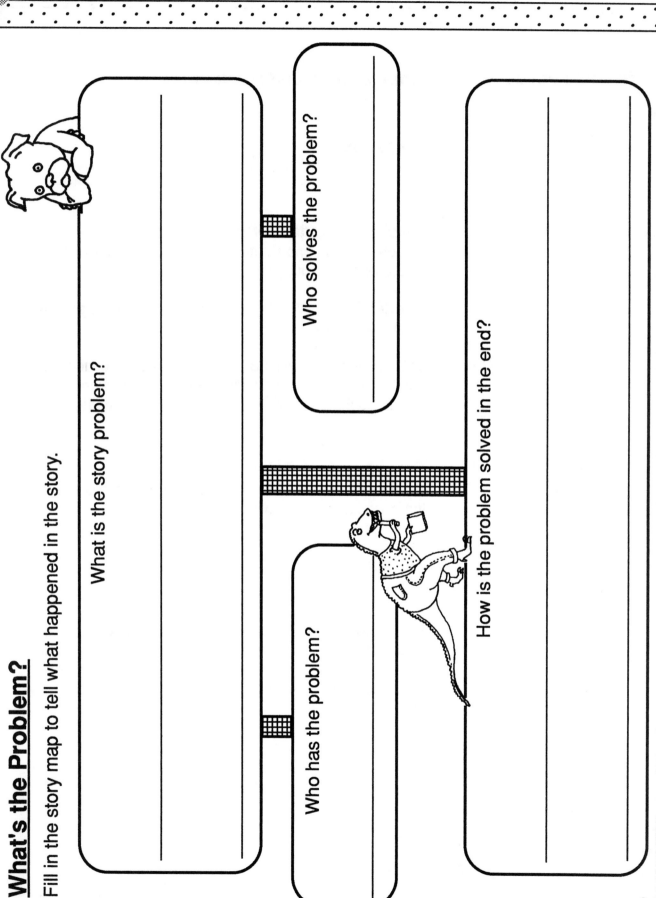

What is the story problem?

Who has the problem?

Who solves the problem?

How is the problem solved in the end?

Complete a story map

Reading Focus   *plot - problem and solution*

Writing Focus   *sentences*

Teaching Suggestions

Review problem and solution by having students identify the problems and solutions in familiar stories.

To extend the activity, have students use their maps to write a story summary.

ESL students: Help students understand the concept of problem - solution by providing examples with wordless picture books, sketches of familiar stories, or pantomime.

Oral Language Activity

Have students rehearse and read aloud the part of the story that introduces the problem and the characters.

Extension Activity

Art

Have students design problem-solving buttons for a main character in the story to wear. On the button, they should create a colorful design and write a saying that tells something about the problem-solving in the story, i.e., *Keep Trying Until You Win.*

Name

Where Will It End?

Help Katie Kangaroo write a different ending for the story.
Make the new ending fit with the rest of the story.

Revise and edit your story ending. Write your final copy on separate paper.

Revise & Edit

Copy

5

Write a story ending

Reading Focus   *predictions*
                    plot - solution

Writing Focus   *story ending*

Teaching Suggestions

Explain that a story ending must be a logical solution to the problem. Have students suggest logical and illogical endings for a familiar story. Discuss why some outcomes do not fit with the story problem or with the character's actions or personality.

ESL students: Have students brainstorm alternate solutions in both languages, especially in their native language. Depending on students' English proficiency, allow them to present their story endings in ways other than writing, i.e., have them act out their endings or draw pictures or cartoons.

Oral Language Activity

Have students briefly retell the main events of the story, except the ending, and then present both their endings and the author's. The members of the audience will decide which ending they prefer.

Extension Activity

Art

Have students illustrate their story endings. Provide a variety of art materials.

Name

Tune In

Suppose one of the most important events in the story is being shown on the TV news. Draw a picture of the event you would see on TV.

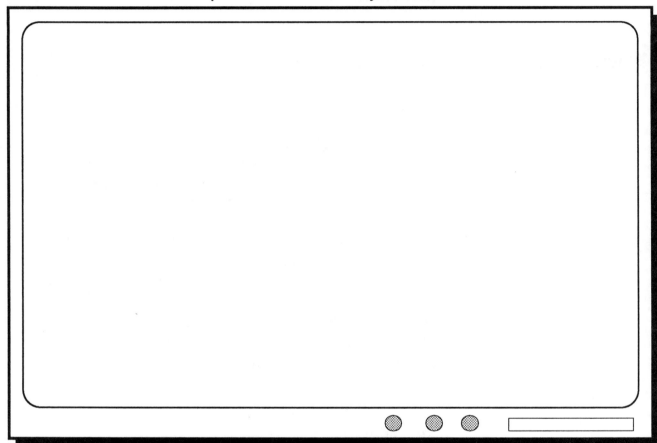

Brenda Bear is a TV news reporter. Help her write a sentence that tells about the event that people are seeing on the TV screen.

Illustrate an important event

Reading Focus   *plot - main event*
                           main idea

Writing Focus   *main idea statement*

Teaching Suggestions

Model how to choose the important events in a story by discussing key events in familiar stories, i.e., the Billy Goats Gruff knocking the troll off the bridge.

Explain that the sentence in the speech bubble should tell what is happening on the screen.

Oral Language Activity

Have students take the role of a TV news broadcaster and give a news report about the event on their TV screens. Explain that the news report should tell the important facts about the event.

ESL students: Allow students to broadcast their news report in their native language to demonstrate understanding and expose the rest of the class to a "global" view of the event. Have the rest of the class translate the news story.

Extension Activity

Social Studies / Science

Have students do the *Tune In* activity with a key idea or event from their current social studies or science unit.

What Happened?

Tell three important events that retell the story.
Write each event in the story map. Write the
events in story order.

EVENTS

First, _____

_____

_____

Next, _____

_____

_____

Last, _____

_____

_____

 On separate paper, write a paragraph to retell the story.

Map and summarize a story

Reading Focus   *plot - main events*
                     sequence

Writing Focus   *summary*

Teaching Suggestions
Suggest students choose one event from the beginning, middle, and the end of the story. Then explain that students should use the events in their maps as the basis for their summaries.

Some students may enjoy drawing a three-panel cartoon to show the events in their maps.

ESL students: Pair ESL students with students who can speak the students' native language. Have each pair work together to complete one story map and summary.

Oral Language Activity
Have students rehearse and read aloud their favorite parts of the story.

Extension Activity

Science
Have students complete a sequence map to show the key steps in a science activity or experiment they will do or have done in class. For example, they might make a map to show the steps they will take to plant seeds.

Plot

Name

Moving Pictures

Follow the directions to make a filmstrip that retells the story.

(1) In the boxes on the filmstrip, draw four pictures that retell the story.

      Box A - Show what happened in the beginning of the story.

      Box B - Show an important event from the middle of the story.

      Box C - Show another important event from the middle of the story.

      Box D - Show what happened at the end.

(2) Decorate the picture frame.

(3) Cut out the frame. Make two slits in the center. Follow the dotted lines.

(4) Cut out the filmstrip. Follow the dotted lines.

(5) Retell the story to a partner as you pull each picture through the frame.

frame

frame

filmstrip

A

B

C

filmstrip

D

11

Make a filmstrip

Reading Focus

plot - beginning, middle, end
plot summary

Teaching Suggestions
Read aloud the directions to be sure students understand each step. Demonstrate how to cut out the filmstrip and frame and how to pull the strip through the frame.

ESL students: To extend the activity, have students make a unique interpretation of the story by adding cultural characteristics to their filmstrip. For example, students may set the story in their native country.

Oral Language Activity
Have each student retell the story to a partner or small group as he or she pulls the filmstrip through the frame.

ESL students: Allow students to retell the story in their native language.

Extension Activity

Social Studies / Science
Have students work in **cooperative group**s to create a filmstrip to illustrate new information learned in a current social studies or science unit.

Headline News

Choose a main event from the beginning, middle, and end of the story. Write each event as a news headline.

Story Title

Beginning

Daily Story

Middle

Daily Story

End

Daily Story

Write headlines

Reading Focus   *plot - main events*
main idea

Writing Focus   *main idea statements*

Teaching Suggestions

Explain that a news headline attracts the attention of the
reader and tells what happened. Refer to the example on
the students' page: *Billy Goats Gruff Beat Tricky Troll.*
Then work with students to formulate headlines based on
events in familiar stories or nursery rhymes, i.e., *Glass
Slipper Found on Palace Steps* or *Little Lamb Lost.*

ESL students: Students who have attended school in
their home countries are familiar with *Cinderella, The Three
Little Pigs*, and other classic fairy tales. When introducing
the concept of headlines and main ideas, have ESL students work with others who speak their language and formulate headlines for fairy tales in their native language.

Oral Language Activity

Have students work in **cooperative groups** to present a
television news broadcast. One student will be the anchor
person and the others, reporters.   Reporters will each
choose one of their headlines and give a brief news report
about the event.

Extension Activity

Science

Have students invent headlines that state main ideas about
information in their current science unit, i.e., *Year Has Four
Seasons* or *Tadpoles Become Frogs.*

Send a Postcard (part 1)

Pretend to be the main character of the story. Write a post card to a friend. Tell your friend what you have been doing. Your note should tell about an event in the story. Then draw a stamp for your post card.

Post Card

To:

Dear _____,

Your friend,

_____

Write a post card note

Reading Focus	*plot - main event*
Writing Focus	*letter* *point of view*

Teaching Suggestions

You may use this response activity alone or in conjunction with the post card-writing activity on page 17.

To introduce the concept of writing from the point of view of a character, read aloud *The Jolly Postman* and discuss how the authors wrote letters from the points of view of various characters.

After students do this activity and the one on page 17, have them make their own post cards from tag board. Before writing their final copies, have students work with partners to revise and edit their notes.

ESL students: Pair limited English proficient students with English dominant students for this activity. Have the English dominant students model the activity and help with vocabulary and sentence structure.

Oral Language Activity

Have students read aloud their post card notes to each other.

Extension Activity

Writing

Have all students put their post cards into a delivery bag. Appoint a student to act as mail carrier and distribute cards at random to the class. Each student will then take the role of the friend receiving the card and write a response to it. A second mail carrier can deliver the responses to the appropriate students.

Name _____

Send a Postcard (part 2)

Draw a picture for the front of your post card. Your picture should show something from the story. Write a title for your picture.

(title)

Design a post card

Reading Focus   *plot - main event*

Teaching Suggestions
This response activity is an optional second part of the post card-writing activity on page 15.

After students do this activity and the one on page 15, have them make their own post cards from tag board.

Oral Language Activity
Have students describe their pictures to a small group or the class.

ESL students: Have English dominant students work in pairs with limited English proficient students to help them with vocabulary to describe their pictures.

Name

Make a Book Cover

Make a cover for a book that contains the story you read. Write the title of the story on your cover. Then draw a picture that will make someone want to read the book. Show the story problem or an exciting event.

Design a book cover

Reading Focus

plot - story problem
plot - exciting event

Teaching Suggestions

Discuss with students the criteria for an inviting book cover: one that captures the reader's interest but doesn't give away the ending. Have students suggest book cover pictures for familiar stories and discuss how their suggestions meet the criteria.

Some students may enjoy making final copies of their book covers on art paper folded like a book jacket.

ESL students: Students who have attended school in their home countries are familiar with classic fairy tales such as *Snow White* and *Cinderella*. Have ESL students work with others who speak their native language to brainstorm picture topics for book covers in their native language.

Oral Language Activity

Have students show the class their covers and give short book talks about their stories. Remind students that like the cover design, a book talk should capture the listener's interest but not reveal how events turn out.

Extension Activity

Writing

Have students write the copy for the flap of a book jacket. Explain that the information on the book flap tells enough about the story to interest the reader. It introduces the characters, tells the problem, and hints at the exciting events that will follow. Students may write their final copies on the flaps of book jackets they make.

Sum It Up

Complete the sentences to retell the story.

The main characters in the story are _____

and _____.   When the story begins,

the problem is _____

_____

_____

_____.

In the middle of the story, _____

tries to solve the problem by _____

_____

_____.

Also, _____

_____

_____.

In the end, the problem is solved when _____

_____

_____.

Complete paragraph frames

Reading Focus

plot - summary
plot - beginning, middle, end

Writing Focus

summary

Teaching Suggestions

Review that a plot summary includes only the most important events that retell the story.

ESL students: Help students understand the concept of plot and its elements by providing examples through wordless picture books, cartoons or sketches of stories, filmstrips, or by having students act out parts of familiar stories.

Oral Language Activity

Have students read their story summaries to a partner.

Extension Activity

Creative Dramatics

Have students work in groups to plan, rehearse, and give story theater presentations of the story. Students should use their summaries as a basis for their presentations.

Name _____

What's News? (part 1)

Pretend to be a newspaper reporter. Write a newspaper story about something that happened in the story.

Reporters collect facts before they write their stories. List the facts for your news story on the notebook page.

THE FACTS

Who did it? _____

What happened? _____

_____

_____

When did it happen? _____

Where did it happen? _____

Why or **how** did it happen? _____

_____

_____

Write your news story on page 2 of this activity.

List key facts

Reading Focus	*plot - main event* *facts - who, what, when, where, why or how*
Writing Focus	*list*

Teaching Suggestions

You may use this response activity alone or in conjunction with the news story-writing activity on page 25.

Discuss the elements of the lead paragraph of a news story and read examples aloud. Have students identify the facts important to include in a news story about an event in a familiar story, i.e., the wolf eating two of the three little pigs.

ESL students: Pair limited English proficient students with English dominant students to work together to locate key facts.

Oral Language Activity

Have students use their facts to tell their news stories to the class.

Extension

Science

Have students list facts for the lead paragraph of a news story about something they are studying in their current science unit.

Name

What's News? (part 2)

Write your news story. Use your list of facts. Then write
a headline for your story. Remember that a headline
tells what your story is about.

| SPECIAL EDITION! | THE NewsPaper | Read All About It! |

HEADLINE

NEWS STORY

EDIT & REVISE

COPY

Edit and revise your story. Write your final copy on separate paper.

Write a news story

Reading Focus	*plot - main event* *main idea*
Writing Focus	*news story* *point of view*

Teaching Suggestions

This response activity is an optional second part of the prewriting activity on page 23.

Before the students begin, explain that a news headline attracts the attention of the reader and states what happened. Read examples and then work with students to formulate headlines based on events in familiar stories, i.e., *Wolf Downs Two Pigs* or *Tortoise Takes First Place*.

Students may wish to draw a picture to accompany the final copies of their news stories.

ESL students: Depending on students' stage of English development, you may wish to have limited English proficient students draw pictures or a cartoon panel instead of writing a news story

Oral Language Activity

Have students work in **cooperative groups** to plan and present a news broadcast. Have one student act as the anchor person and the others as network reporters.

Extension Activity

Writing

Have students work in **cooperative groups** to create the front page of the ***Literature News***, a paper that tells about favorite stories. Each group member will contribute a news story about an event in his or her favorite story. Encourage students to design a creative masthead .

©Spring-Street Press

Name _____

Map It

Complete the story map. First, tell the problem. Then tell about one or two important things that happened in the middle of the story.   Last, tell how the problem was solved.

PROBLEM

_____

_____

_____

WHAT HAPPENED IN THE MIDDLE OF THE STORY?

_____

_____

_____

_____

_____

SOLUTION

_____

_____

On separate paper, write a paragraph to retell the story.

Map and summarize a story

© Spring-Street Press

Reading Focus   *plot - elements*

Writing Focus   *plot summary*

Teaching Suggestions

Review the elements of a plot: problem, key events in the rising action, and the solution. Remind students that they should choose only the most important events to retell the rising action.

ESL students: Help students understand the concept of plot and its elements by providing examples through word-less picture books, pictures from familiar stories, filmstrips, or by acting out familiar stories.

Oral Language Activity

Have students take the role of storytellers and use their plot maps to retell the story.

Extension Activity

Creative Dramatics

Have students work in **cooperative groups** to plan and present the story as a puppet show.   First, students will make puppets by drawing faces on tongue depressors. Then they will take turns retelling the story while the other group members manipulate the puppets.

ESL students: Encourage ESL students to add cultural characteristics to make their puppet shows unique. For example, the setting of the puppet show may be changed to the student's home country.

© Spring-Street Press

Name

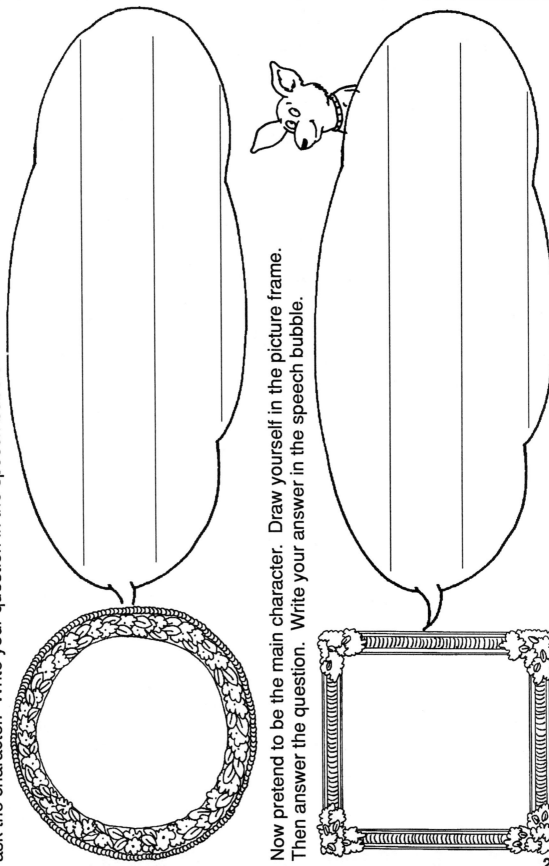

Ask and Answer

Imagine that you met the main character of the story. Draw a picture of yourself in the picture frame. Then write a question that you would ask the character. Write your question in the speech bubble.

Now pretend to be the main character. Draw yourself in the picture frame. Then answer the question. Write your answer in the speech bubble.

Write a question and answer

Reading Focus   *conclusions*

Writing Focus   *questions and answers*
                           point of view

Teaching Suggestions

Explain to students that when they assume the role of
the character and answer the question, they should think
like the character. Remind students to write their answers in the first person.

ESL students: Pair limited English proficiency students
with English dominant students for this activity. Have
the English dominant student provide a model for writing
and saying questions and answers as well as help with
vocabulary and sentence structure.

Oral Language Activity

Have students work in **cooperative groups** to prepare
and present a television talk show entitled *"A Talk with
the Characters."* One group member will be the show
host and ask questions; the others will assume the roles
of their characters and answer the questions. Remind
students to base their talk shows on their questions and
answers.

Extension Activity

Writing

Have students write additional questions for their character and then answer them. If students have read the
same story, they may wish to answer each other's questions.

Name

Button, Button

Often people wear buttons that have messages on them.

Make a button for a character in the story. The message on the button should tell something about the character. Or, it should tell what lesson the character learned.

Then use pens or crayons to make a design to go with the message.

Whose button will you design?

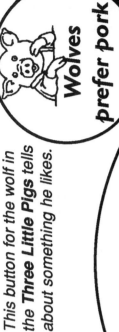

*This button for the wolf in the **Three Little Pigs** tells about something he likes.*

Little Red Riding Hood's button tells the lesson she learned in the story.

Write a button message

Reading Focus	*conclusion - character traits* *theme*
Writing Focus	*slogans*

Teaching Suggestions

Before students begin, discuss the examples of button messages on the activity page. Then have students brainstorm possible messages that would be appropriate for other fairy tale characters. Make two lists: one with messages that tell about character's traits and one that tells the lessons characters learned. Explain that either type of message is appropriate.

Provide pens or crayons for students to use to decorate their buttons.

ESL students: Have ESL students brainstorm slogans in both languages. Then have them discuss their slogans with English dominant students who then can help with vocabulary and spelling.

Oral Language Activity

Have students show their buttons to the class, tell their messages, and then explain why the message is appropriate for the character.

Extension Activity

Health

Have students create button messages that relate concepts they are learning in health, i.e.: *Keep Teeth Healthy - Brush and Floss, Green vegetables are great* .

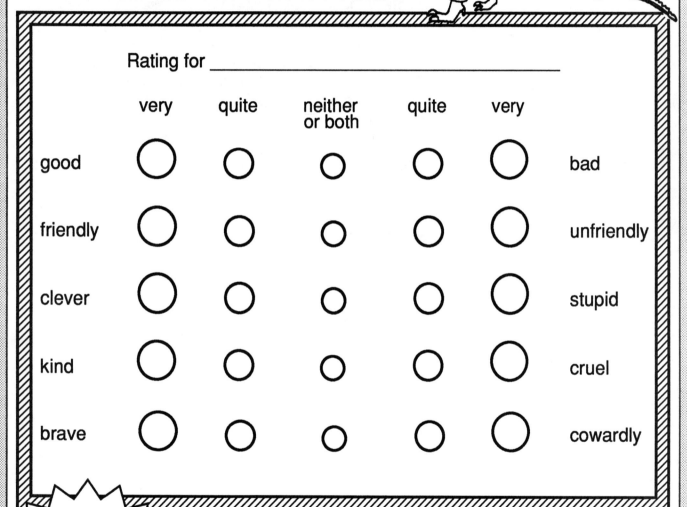

Name

Give an Award

Help Diana Dinosaur decide who wins the **Character of the Month** award. Rate the main character of the story. Color one circle in each row that best describes the character. Then decide if the character should receive the award.

Rating for _____

	very	quite	neither or both	quite	very	
good	○	○	○	○	○	bad
friendly	○	○	○	○	○	unfriendly
clever	○	○	○	○	○	stupid
kind	○	○	○	○	○	cruel
brave	○	○	○	○	○	cowardly

Character of the Month

_____ should / should not

receive the **Character of the Month** Award because

_____

_____

Rate a character

© Spring Street Press

Reading Focus

inferences - character traits
judgements

Teaching Suggestions

Before students begin, explain how to use the chart to rate a character. Point out that the words on each line are opposites and that positive traits are listed down the left of the paper and their negatives, down the right. Remind students that if the author does not directly comment on a specific trait, they will have to infer the trait. Therefore, to rate a character who is mean and nasty, students will move to the right in the *kind - cruel* category.

Explain that when a character does not exhibit one of the traits or exhibits both at different times in the story, they will shade in the middle circle under "neither or both."

ESL students: Help students understand the concept each word conveys by providing examples through pictures or pantomime. Also be sure students understand that words in each category are opposites.

Oral Language Activity

Ask students to explain why they rated their characters as they did.

Extension Activity

Writing

Have students use the information in their charts to write paragraphs that describe their characters.

Tell About a Character

Complete the map to tell about your favorite character in the story.

Character's Name

List four words that describe the character.

1

2

3

4

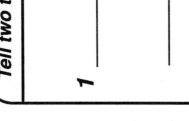

Tell two things the character likes to do.

1

2

On separate paper, write a description of the character. Use the information in your map.

Describe a character

Reading Focus *conclusions - character traits*

Writing Focus *character sketch*

Teaching Suggestions

Explain that some of the words students use to describe their characters should tell about the character's personality. Then have them brainstorm words they might use to describe familiar story characters, i.e., the third little pig in *The Three Little Pigs* is hardworking, clever, and sensible. Remind students that they may have to infer a character's traits from things the character says and does.

Students may wish to draw a picture of the character to accompany their written sketches.

ESL students: Have ESL students brainstorm words that describe characters in both languages and then work with English dominant students to translate the words they want to use for the activity. Depending on the students' English proficiency, allow them to describe their characters by acting out their traits instead of writing a character sketch.

Oral Language Activity

Have students give oral character sketches. Students will use their maps as a basis for their descriptions.

Extension Activity

Writing

Have students make greeting cards for family members or close friends. Students will complete a map to describe the person who will receive the card. Then they will use pens or crayons to design a card on art paper and use the information in the charts to write a message in the card.

Dear Helpful Helen (part 1)

Pretend to be the main character in the story. Write to Helpful Helen. Tell her about one of your problems and ask her for help.

_____ **(date)**

Dear Helpful Helen,

_____

_____

_____

_____

_____

_____

_____

_____

Yours truly,

_____

Write a letter

Reading Focus   *conclusions - character problems*

Writing Focus   *explanation*
point of view

Teaching Suggestions

You may use this response activity alone or in conjunction with the letter-writing activity on page 39. After
writing his or her letter to Helpful Helen, have the student
take the role of Helpful Helen and do the letter-writing
activity on page 39. A second option is to have another
student in the class take the role of Helpful Helen and do
the letter-writing activity on page 39.

Before students begin, explain the *Dear Abby* column
and read some examples. Tell students that they will be
taking the role of a character in the story and writing a
letter to Helpful Helen asking her for advice.

ESL students: Pair ESL students with classmates who
can speak the student's native language. Have pairs
work on one letter together.

Oral Language Activity

Have students read aloud their letters to partners.

Name

Dear Helpful Helen (part 2)

Helpful Helen always helps her writers with their problems. Imagine that you are Helpful Helen. Answer the letter that you wrote her.

_____
date

Dear _____

_____

_____

_____

_____

_____

_____

_____

Sincerely,
Helpful Helen

Write a letter of advice

Reading Focus   *judgements*

Writing Focus   *opinions*
                           point of view

Teaching Suggestions
This response activity is an optional second part of the letter-writing activity on page 37. You may wish to have students complete this letter after they write the one on page 37. Or another student may write this letter in response to a classmate's letter from the activity on page 37.

Have students work with a partner to revise and edit their letters and write final copies on stationery.

ESL students: Pair ESL students with classmates who can speak the students' native language. Have pairs work on one letter together.

Oral Language Activity
Have students present a radio talk show in which book characters call Helpful Helen to discuss their problems. The content of the talk show should be based on the problems and solutions students wrote about in their letters.

Extension Activity

Math
Have students write letters to Millie Mathematics asking her for help with math problems they find difficult. Have students exchange letters, solve the problems, and write letters back that give the solutions and an explanation of how they arrived at the solutions.

Name

Tee Shirt Talk

Write a saying for a tee shirt that your favorite character in the story might wear. Your saying should tell something about the character. Then decorate the shirt.

My favorite character is _____

Write a tee shirt slogan

Reading Focus   *conclusions - character traits and motives*

Writing Focus   *slogans*

Teaching Suggestions

Discuss what characters in familiar stories might wear the slogan on the toad's tee shirt. Then have students brainstorm slogans that would be appropriate for other fairy tale characters. For example, a slogan for a tee shirt for a dwarf in *Snow White* might be "Little People Have Big Hearts" and "Bigfoot Lives" for Cinderella's stepmother.

Provide pens or crayons for students to use to decorate their tee shirts.

ESL students: Have ESL students brainstorm slogans in both languages. Then have them discuss their slogans with English dominant students who can help with vocabulary and spelling.

Oral Language Activity

Have students show their tee shirt drawings to the class, tell their slogans, and then explain why their slogans are appropriate for the characters.

Extension Activities

Writing

Have students write a sentence or paragraph that explains why their slogans are appropriate for the characters.

Social Studies

Have students write tee shirt slogans for people they are currently studying.

Name

Figure Out a Character

Write the answers to the questions on the lines.

1. Who is one of the important characters in the story?

_____

Word List

brave
selfish
hardworking
kind
wicked
wise
funny
foolish
determined
thoughtful
mean
careless

2. Choose a word from the **Word List** that best describes

   your character. Or choose another word you know.

   Write the word here. _____

   Now, write the word in three places marked 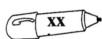.

3. Write one thing that the character does that shows that

   he or she is _____ 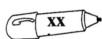 .

   _____

   _____.

4. Write one thing that the character says that shows that

   he or she is _____ 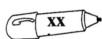.

   "_____

   _____."

5. Think of some other characters in stories you have read.

   Who else is _____ ?

Favorite Stories

   Write the character's name here. _____

Describe a character

Reading Focus   *conclusions - character traits*

Writing Focus   *sentences*
     quotation

Teaching Suggestions

Explain that often writers do not directly state a character's personalty traits. Instead they reveal a character's traits by what the character says and does. In this activity, students will identify what a character says and does to reveal one of his or her personality traits.

ESL students: Help students understand the concept of character traits by providing examples with pictures or by acting. Check understanding by having students brainstorm common character traits in both languages. Then have students work with English dominant students to complete the response activity.

Oral Language Activity

Have students give one or two minute talks in which they describe their character. Students should use the information on their response sheets for the content of their talks.

Extension Activity

Writing

Have students use the information on the response sheet as the basis of a paragraph that describes one of the story character's personality traits and explains how the character reveals that trait. Use the paragraph frame below to help students.

_____ is _____. I know this because he/she _____
_____. Also, he/she says _____
_____.

44

© Spring Street Press

Come to a Party

Pretend that you are a story character who is giving a birthday party. Make a list of names of the other story characters you will invite. Then write an invitation to your favorite guest.

Who will be invited

1 _____

2 _____

3 _____

4 _____

5 _____

Dear _____,

Please come to my birthday party.

Date: _____

Time: _____

Place: _____

Hope you will be there.

From, _____

(character's name)

Write a party invitation

Reading Focus

characters
setting

Writing Focus

list
point of view

Teaching Suggestions

Remind students that when they pretend to be a character, they should think like the character. For example, the time and place of the party should be consistent with where the character would be likely to have the party.

Oral Language Activity

Have students work in pairs to practice and present an imaginary telephone conversation of the character asking a guest to the party. Students will use the information on their invitations. Help students with telephone etiquette. If possible, supply two telephones for students to use when they present their conversations.

ESL students: Help ESL students create, practice, and present a conversation in which they use phrases that are common in telephone conversations, i.e., this is _____, may I speak with _____, is _____ there, may I take a message, tell ____ that I called, etc.

Extension Activity

Art

Have students design and make invitations with construction paper, pens, and crayons. Have them decorate the invitations with a design that is consistent with the story plot or setting. Make a bulletin board display of students' invitations.

Name

Paper Plate Puppet

You can turn a paper plate into almost any story character just by using your imagination.

Choose a favorite story character. Then change a paper plate into a hand puppet of your character. On this paper, draw how you will make your puppet.

Puppet's name _____

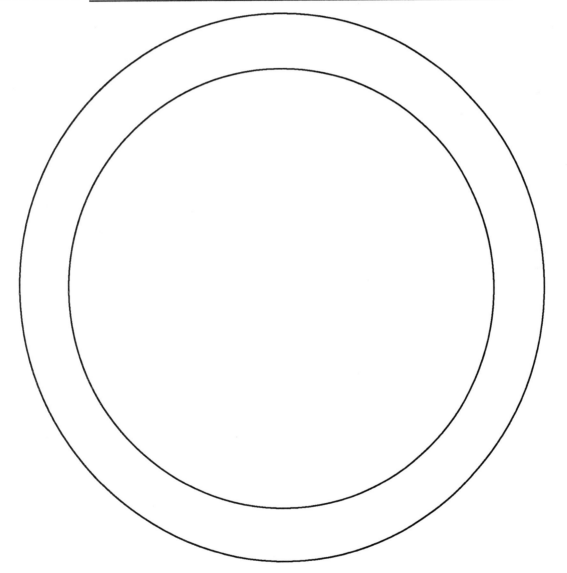

Now use a paper plate to make your puppet.
Paste the plate onto a stick so you can hold it.

Make a puppet

Reading Focus   *character traits*

Teaching Suggestions

Have students design their puppets on the page and then construct them with paper plates. Explain to students that they will draw and color the character's basic features on the plate. Encourage them to pay special attention to features that show a character's traits. Present materials students may use to attach to the plate, i.e., construction paper for floppy dog ears or pipe cleaners for cat whiskers. Provide tongue depressors for students to paste to the plates so they can hold their puppets.

Oral Language Activity

Have students use their puppets to retell their favorite part of the story. Encourage students to retell the story from their character's point of view, i.e., tell *The Three Billy Goats Gruff* from the troll's point of view.

ESL students: Allow students to retell their favorite parts of the story in their native language.

Extension Activity

Science / Social Studies

Have students use their puppets to explain science or social studies concepts they are studying.

Name

What a Character!

Choose a character from the story. Describe the character by completing the story map.

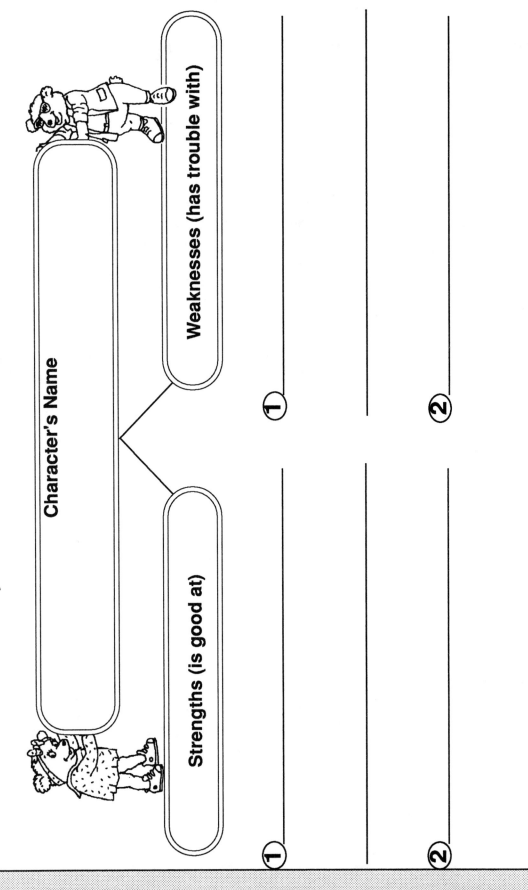

Character's Name

Strengths (is good at)

①

②

Weaknesses (has trouble with)

①

②

➤ On separate paper, write a description of the character. Use the information in your map.

Map character traits

Reading Focus   *conclusions - character traits*

Writing Focus   *paragraph*

Teaching Suggestions

Discuss the strengths and weaknesses of familiar story characters. Then have students brainstorm other words that describe people's strengths and weaknesses.

Suggest that when students write their descriptions, they first discuss the character's strengths and then his or her weaknesses.

ESL students: Have ESL students brainstorm words that describe strengths and weaknesses in both English and their native language. Depending on students' English proficiency, allow them to present their character descriptions in some way other than writing a paragraph, i.e., through skits or pictures.

Oral Language Activity

Have students describe their characters. Suggest that they first tell about the characters' strengths and then their weaknesses.

Extension

Social Studies

Have students work in **cooperative groups** to suggest things characters could do to strengthen their weaknesses.

Name

Magic Mirror

Choose a word from the Word List to describe your favorite story character. Or choose another word of your own. Write your word and your character's name to complete the **Magic Words**. Then draw your character's picture in the **Magic Mirror**.

Word List

bravest
scariest
funniest
smartest
kindest
strangest
meanest
strongest
nicest
sweetest
prettiest
wickedest

MAGIC WORDS

Mirror, mirror, on the wall.

Who's the _____ **one of all?**

The magic mirror answers, "It's _____**."**

(character)

51

Describe and draw a character

© Spring Street Press

Reading Focus   *conclusions - character traits*

Teaching Suggestions
Have students brainstorm other words they might choose to describe their characters. Remind students that if an author does not directly state a character's traits, they will have to infer those traits by thinking about the character's actions, words, and thoughts.

ESL students: Have ESL students work in groups with English dominant students to learn the words in the Word List. Have students convey the meanings of words through pictures and acting.

Oral Language Activity
Have students take the role of the Magic Mirror and hold up the picture of their character and say, "(Character's name) is the (descriptive word) of all." Then ask them to tell why that word suits the character.

Extension Activity

Science
Use this response activity with the study of light energy.

Discuss with students the concept of reflection (the return of a light wave after it strikes a surface). Compare reflection to the action of a ball rebounding from a wall. Ask students to explain why mirrors are reflectors - objects that cause light to bounce back. Then have students work in **cooperative groups** to identify reflectors they see in the world around them, i.e., reflectors on bicycles or road signs, water, polished surfaces. Discuss how and why people use different types of reflectors.

Name

Missing! (part 1)

The main character of the story is missing and must be found! Complete the *Missing Character Report* to help the police find the character.

Missing Character Report

Name _____

Type of creature (human, bear, cat, etc.) _____

Eyes _____ Hair _____

Size _____

Special Features (What will help someone recognize the character?)

_____

_____

Clothing (What was the character wearing last time he or she was seen?)

_____

Habits (What does the character usually do?)

_____

_____

Last seen: Where? _____

When? _____

Complete a missing person report

Reading Focus

conclusions - character traits
facts

Teaching Suggestions

You may use this response activity alone or in conjunction with the poster-making activity on page 55.

Help students understand that they should include information on the report that are clues to the character's whereabouts. For example, for Little Red Riding Hood, habits might include walking through the woods alone.

Oral Language Activity

Have students work in pairs to create and present an interview that might take place between a police officer filling out the missing character report and an interested friend who is giving the information. Students will use their missing character reports for their questions and answers.

ESL students: Have ESL students work in pairs with English dominant students to prepare for the interview. For example, an English dominant student and an ESL student both playing a police officer would work together to practice asking questions; and the interested friends would work together on answers. Then have each pair present their interview.

Extension Activity

Science
Have students complete a missing character report for an animal they are studying in science.

Name

Missing! (part 2)

Make a poster to help find the missing character. Draw a picture of the character. Then write a short description of him or her. Turn the information from your report into sentences.

Missing!

Reward! $_____

Name _____

Description _____

_____

_____

_____

_____

Last seen _____
(when and where)

_____

Make a missing person poster

Reading Focus   *conclusions - character traits*

Writing Focus   *description*

Teaching Suggestions

This response activity is an optional second part of the missing person report-writing activity on page 53. You may wish to have students do this response activity after they do part 1 as a prewriting activity.

Remind students to use the information in their missing character report as a basis for their descriptions. Model how to change facts from the report into sentences.

Oral Language Activity

Have students give short television reports in which they describe the missing character and show the character's picture.

ESL students: Allow students to give their reports in their native language. After students give their reports, help the class translate them.

Extension Activity

Writing

Have students write short stories that relate the events that led up to the character's status as "missing," or one that tells how he or she was found. Students may tell their stories to the class.

Name

What Did They Want?

Stories usually tell about characters who want something very much. Complete this story chart to tell what the characters in the story wanted and how they tried to get what they wanted.

Character	What the Character Wanted	What the Character Did to Get It
1.		
2.		
3.		

Which character or characters got what they wanted? Circle the name or names in the chart.

Complete a story chart

Reading Focus   *conclusions - character goals*

Teaching Suggestions

Explain that most stories are about characters' goals and how they go about achieving them. Some characters achieve their goals and others don't. Use characters in familiar stories as examples.

Point out to students that they will write one goal or action in each box on the chart.

ESL students: Depending on students' stage of English development, you may wish to have limited English proficient students draw pictures to illustrate goals and characters' actions to obtain them.

Oral Language Activity

Have students choose one character from their chart, tell his or her goal, and relate two or three things the character did to achieve his or her goal.

Extension Activity

Social Studies

Have students complete a similar chart for themselves and two family members.

Name

What a Knight

Long ago knights wore symbols called coats of arms. Pictures on the coat of arms showed important things about the person who wore it.

Design a coat of arms for the main character of the story.   Draw two pictures. In one picture, show the character's best quality. In the other, show an important event in the character's life.

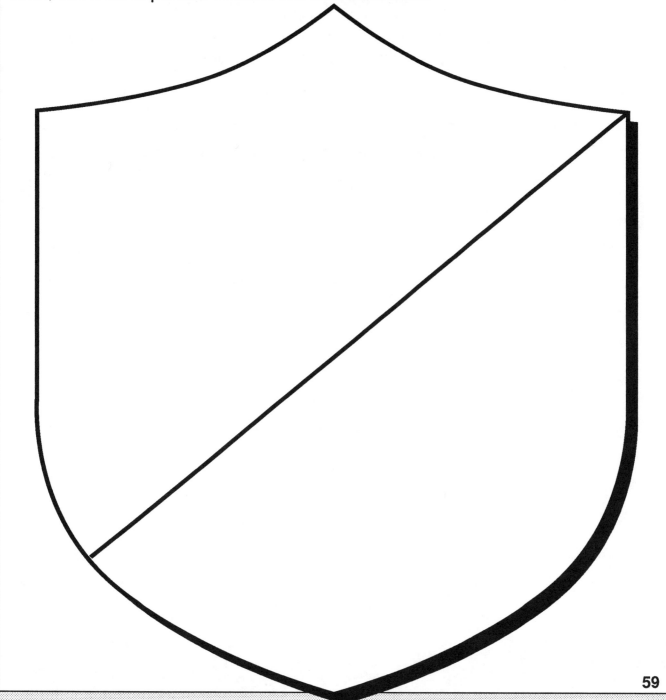

Design a coat of arms

Reading Focus

conclusions - character traits
main event

Teaching Suggestions

Explain how symbols may represent character traits. For example, a lion might symbolize power, or a balloon, happiness. Encourage students to think of original symbols to represent their character's best quality.

Some students may wish to draw final copies of their coats of arms on art paper.

ESL students: To introduce the class to students' culture and to provide further examples of symbols, ask ESL students to describe or draw symbols that their culture uses.

Oral Language Activity

Have students show their coats of arms to the class and explain their designs.

Extension Activity

Social Studies

Have students make coats of arms for themselves. Students' coats of arms should show their best quality and the most important event in their lives.

Name _____

How Did You Feel?

Pretend to be the main character of the story. Complete the sentences to tell how you felt during the story.

I am _____. In the beginning
(character)

of the story, I felt _____. In the middle, I felt

_____. At the end, I felt

_____.

Draw a picture that shows how you felt at the end of the story.
Remember that you are the main character of the story.

Write a title for your picture

[   ]

Describe character feelings

Reading Focus   *conclusions - character feelings*

Writing Focus   *paragraph frame*
                           point of view

Teaching Suggestions

Explain that the author may not directly state how a character feels; therefore, the reader must conclude a character's feelings from what the character says, does, and thinks. For example, when a character slams a door and stomps his feet, we conclude that he is angry; or when a character has butterflies in her stomach, that she is nervous. Then have students brainstorm words that they may use to describe feelings: happy, sad, angry, shy, fearless, concerned, tired, jealous, helpless, cheerful, frightened, etc.

ESL students: Have ESL students work in groups with English dominant students to learn words that express feelings. Begin by having students brainstorm words that express feelings in both English and their native language and recording the words. Then have the group work together to translate all the words into English. Suggest that students act out meanings and draw pictures.

Oral Language Activity

Have students rehearse and read aloud part of the story that reveals how a character feels.

Extension Activity

Creative Dramatics

Have students take the role of the main character and pantomime the feelings of that character during each part of the story.

Name

Be a Story Pen Pal

Pretend to be a character in the story. Write a note to another character.
Tell your pen pal what you think about what happened in the story.

Dear _____,

Yours truly,

_____

Write a letter

Reading Focus   *judgements*

Writing Focus   *opinion*
point of view

Teaching Suggestions

To introduce the activity, read aloud *The Jolly Postman*. Discuss how the authors wrote letters from the points of view of various characters.

You may wish to have students revise and edit their letters and write their final copies on stationery.

ESL students: Pair ESL students with English dominant students. Have each pair write one letter together. Then have ESL students read aloud their letters and have their partners provide coaching.

Oral Language Activity

Have students read aloud their letters to small groups of students.

Extension Activity

Writing

Have students take the role of the character to whom they have written and write a letter of response.

© Spring Street Press

Give Grades

Write a report card for a main character in the story.

• Give the character grades in three subjects.

• Choose three subjects from the list.
Or choose your own.

• Under comments, tell why you gave each grade.

SUBJECTS

honesty
courage
imagination
kindness
friendliness
happiness
cleverness
helpfulness
thoughtfulness

Grades

A Outstanding
B Good
C Satisfactory
D Needs Improvement
F Unsatisfactory

REPORT CARD

for _____
(character's name)

Subject	Grade	Comments

Write a report card

Reading Focus   *conclusions - character traits
                          evaluation*

Writing Focus   *statements to support opinions*

Teaching Suggestions
Read the list of subjects with students and discuss what each means. Point out that the subjects are stated in positive terms; therefore, if students are grading a character whom they feel is nasty, they would choose kindness as the subject and give the character a low grade. Have students brainstorm other subjects to add to the list. Explain that students should choose three subjects that are appropriate for their characters.

ESL students: Help students with the vocabulary in the "subjects" list by giving examples, using pictures, or through acting out word meanings.

Oral Language Activity
Have students work in pairs to role play conferences between the character and the reader. The readers will explain why the characters received the grades they did. If grades are low, the readers and characters should discuss ways to make improvements.

Extension Activity

Health
Have students use the report card format to grade themselves on personal habits they are learning in health. For example, a report card on tooth care might include subjects such as brushing after meals, flossing, visiting the dentist, and eating healthful snacks.

Name

Friends Together

Choose your favorite character from the story. Think about how you and the character are alike. Draw a picture to show you and the character doing something together that you both enjoy. Give your picture a title.

Title:

Draw a picture

Reading Focus

comparisons
main idea

Teaching Suggestions
Remind students that the title of a picture should tell what it is mainly about.

Oral Language Activity
Have students hold up their pictures and tell what they and the character are doing together.

ESL students: Depending on students' English proficiency, allow students to give their oral presentations in their native language.

Extension Activity

Creative Dramatics
Have students work in pairs to prepare a pantomime that shows what they and the characters enjoy doing together.

Name

Who Likes What? (part 1)

Choose your favorite character from the story. Complete the chart to tell how you and the character are alike and different. List three things each of you likes to do.

What I Like to Do

1 _____

2 _____

3 _____

What _____ **Likes to Do**

_____
(character)

1 _____

2 _____

3 _____

Now, complete the sentences on page 2 of this activity. Use the information in your chart.

Complete a chart

Reading Focus   *comparisons and contrasts*
                         conclusions - character traits

Writing Focus   list

Teaching Suggestions

You may use this response activity alone or in conjunction with the writing activity on page 71.

Explain to students that they will draw conclusions about what their favorite character likes to do from his or her actions and thoughts. Encourage students to think of ways they are both similar to and different from the character.

ESL students: Depending on students' English proficiency, allow them to show comparisons and contrasts by drawing pictures or through acting.

Oral Language Activity

Have students tell small groups one way they are like the character and one way they are different from the character.

Extension Activity

Science

Have students use the chart format to compare the features of two plants, animals, or objects that they are studying in science.

Name _____

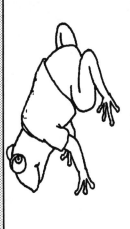

Who Likes What? (part 2)

Complete the sentences to tell how you and the character are alike and different. Use the information in your chart.

1. Both _____ and I like to _____
      (character)

   _____

2. _____ likes to _____
   (character)

   _____

   but I prefer to _____

Now write a sentence of your own. Tell how you and the character are alike or different in one other way.

3. _____

   _____

71

Write sentences

Reading Focus	*comparisons and contrast*
Writing Focus	*sentences - comparison and contrast*

Teaching Suggestions

This response activity is an optional second part of the comparison activity on page 69.

Discuss with students various sentence structures for writing sentences that compare or contrast two things.

ESL students: Have ESL students do the response activity with students who have English as their dominant language.

Oral Language Activity

Have students read aloud their sentences to partners.

Extension Activity

Science

Have students use the sentence formats to write sentences that compare or contrast two animals, plants, or objects they are studying in science.

Name

Poems Make Pictures

1. Draw the picture you imagined as you listened to the poem.

2. Write a word that describes how the
   poem made you feel.

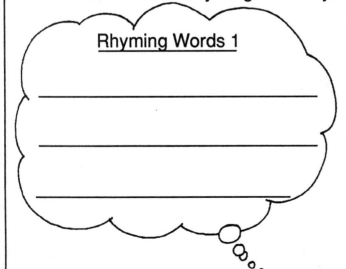

_____

3. Write the rhyming words that you heard in the poem.
   Then add another rhyming word of your own.

Rhyming Words 1

_____

_____

_____

Rhyming Words 2

_____

_____

_____

Respond freely to a poem

Reading Focus

conclusions
rhyming words

Teaching Suggestions

Read the poem aloud several times to students.

Have students do number 3 on the activity page only if there are rhyming words in the poem.

***ESL student*s:** Depending on the stage of their English development, students may not know the word *imagine;* therefore, use alternative wording such as "draw what comes to your mind" or "draw what you think about when you hear the poem."

Oral Language Activity

Have each student rehearse his or her favorite couplet or stanza from the poem and read it aloud.

Extension Activity

Music
Have students choose music that evokes the same feelings as the poem. Read the poem aloud again and play students' musical selections.

Ask a Wheel of Questions

Fill in the wheel with three questions you would like to
ask the author about this story.

Story Title: _____

Author: _____

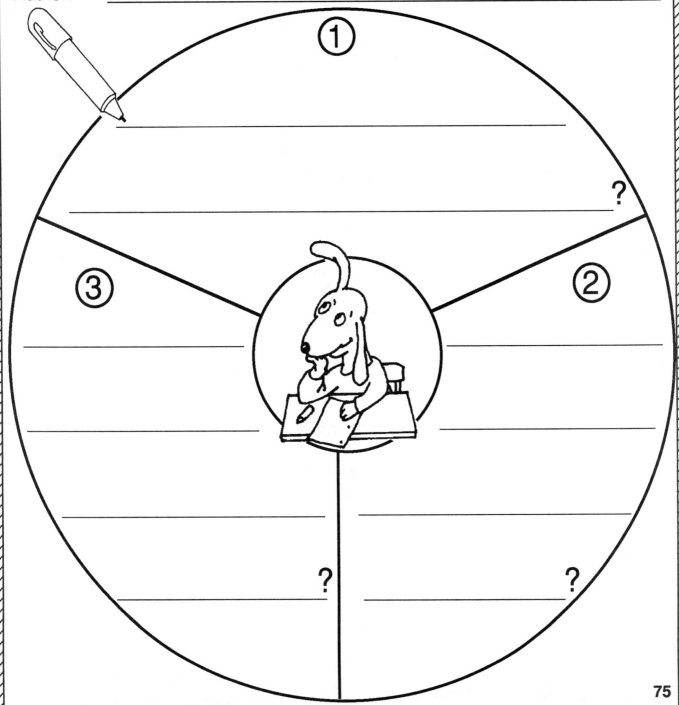

Write questions

Reading Focus	*author's purpose*
Writing Focus	*exposition - questions*

Teaching Suggestions

Have students pretend to be the author and write the answer to one of their questions, or have them tell their answer to a partner.

Oral Language Activity

Have students work in pairs to plan and present a press conference based on their questions. One student will play the reporter; the other, the author. Students will make up answers the author might give.

ESL students: Have students who have the same native language work in pairs to plan and present their press conferences. Allow pairs to present the press conferences in their native language. Have the rest of the class interpret or translate the press conference.

Extension Activity

Writing

Have students write letters to the author and use at least two of their questions in their letters.

General

Name

Fill in the Faces

Draw a face to tell what you thought or felt about each part of the story. Use the faces below as a guide.

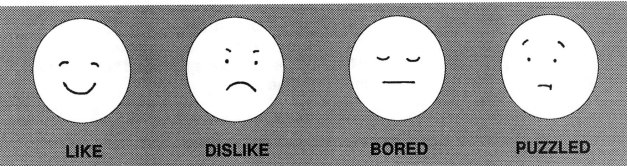

LIKE   DISLIKE   BORED   PUZZLED

1. How did you feel about the main character?

2. Choose another character from the story.

How did you feel about _____?
(character's name)

3. What did you think of the pictures in the story?

4. What did you think of the story?

5. Would you tell a friend to read this story? (Circle one)   **YES**   **NO**
Tell why.

_____

_____

77

© Spring Street Press

Evaluate a story

Reading Focus   *judgements*

Teaching Suggestions
Tell students that they may choose to draw different faces to express feelings different from the four on the page.

Oral Language Activity
Have students choose the part of the story that they liked best and read it aloud to a small group of students. Before students read aloud, allow them time to rehearse. Encourage them to read with expression

ESL students: Listen to ESL students rehearse their passages or pair them with English dominant students for assistance with pronunciation and meaning.

Extension Activity

Art
Have students make a collage that expresses their feelings about the story.

Name _____

Mark That Book

Follow the steps to make a bookmark.

1 In the top of the bookmark pattern, write the title, author, and your name.

2 In the bottom part, draw someone or something from the story. Choose something you enjoyed.

3 Cut out the bookmark. Follow the dotted lines.

4 Fold the bookmark in half along the double line in the middle. Be sure you can see the picture and the printing.

5 Paste the two sides together.

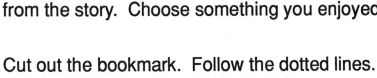

cut

Title _____

_____

Author _____

Name _____

cut

cut

cut

Make a bookmark

Reading Focus

judgement
sequence - directions

Teaching Suggestions

Help the students follow the directions to make their bookmarks.

ESL students: Pair ESL students with English dominant students for help with the directions for making the bookmark. The English dominant student should read each direction aloud and then show the ESL student what to do, repeating the direction as he or she does the step.

Oral Language Activity

Have students rehearse and read aloud the part of the story that inspired their bookmarks.

Extension Activity

Science

Have students make a bookmark for their science textbooks. For their pictures, students should draw something that conveys a key idea that they are studying in science.

Name _____

What's So Funny?

Write the answers to the questions on the lines.

1. How funny was the story?   Color
   the **Laugh Meter** to show your rating.

2. What was the funniest part
   of the story?

   _____

   Why do you think so? _____

   _____

3. Who was the funniest character? _____

   Why do you think so? _____

   _____

4. Would you give this story to a friend who likes funny stories? _____

   If yes, who? _____

5. What is the funniest story that you've ever read?

   _____

Evaluate a humorous story

Reading Focus

humor
judgements

Writing Focus

opinions

Teaching Suggestions

This activity is designed to be used with humorous selections.

Before the students begin, discuss what elements make a story funny. Then show students how to color the Laugh Meter to indicate their ratings.

ESL students: Depending on students' English proficiency, allow them to demonstrate their understanding by drawing pictures rather than writing answers to questions 2 and 3.

Oral Language Activity

Have students each tell one thing that makes them laugh.

Extension Activity

Creative Dramatics

Have students work in groups to plan and present a story theater production of one of the funny scenes from the story.

General

Predict and Read (part 1)

Follow the directions and complete the sentences to help you read the story.

Before You Read

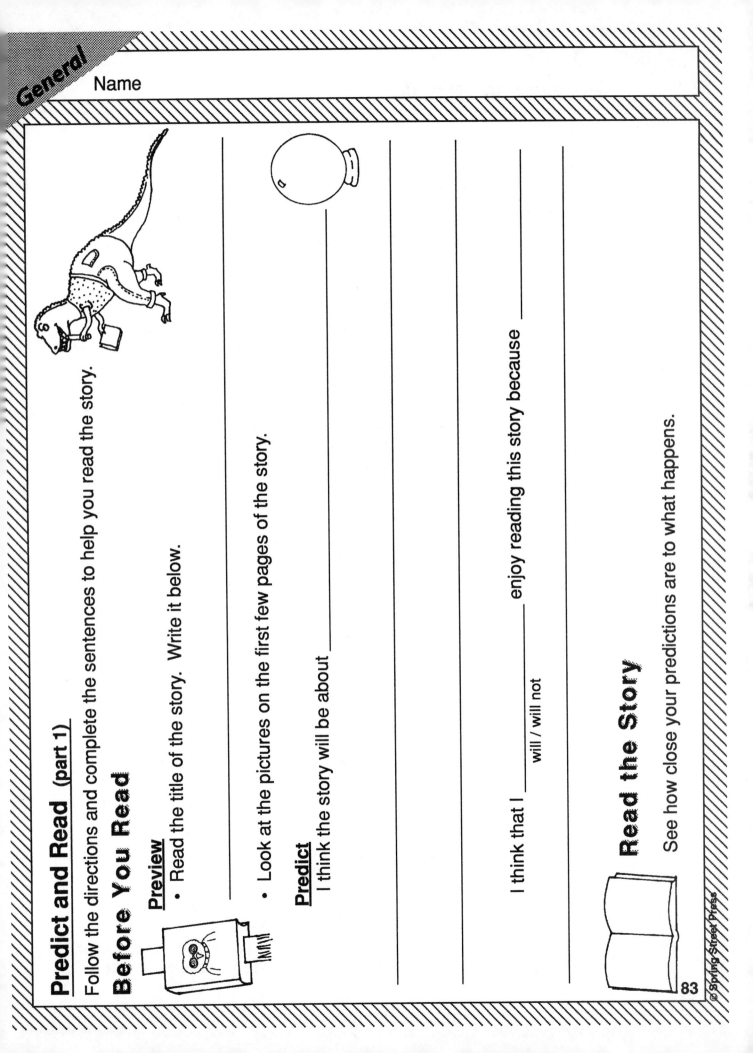

Preview
- Read the title of the story. Write it below.

_____

- Look at the pictures on the first few pages of the story.

Predict
I think the story will be about _____

_____

_____

I think that I _____ enjoy reading this story because _____
         will / will not

_____

Read the Story

See how close your predictions are to what happens.

Preview and predict

Reading Focus   *predictions*

Writing Focus   *paragraph frames*

Teaching Suggestions

You may use this response activity alone or in conjunction with the postreading activity on page 85.

Before students do the response activity, explain what previewing and predicting are, when and why to preview and predict, and then model the strategy with a familiar story.

Stress that there are no "wrong" predictions. Warn students to look only at the first few pictures of fictional stories so they won't learn the story outcome before reading it. However, students should preview an entire nonfiction selection.

ESL students: Help students understand the concept of prediction. Allow students to draw their predictions or use pictures to indicate understanding.

Oral Language Activity

Have students discuss their predictions in small groups. Have each group report the predictions that their group members made.

Extension Activity

Health / Science / Social Studies

Have students do the previewing and predicting activity when they read their content area textbooks.

Predict and Read (part 2)

Complete the sentences.

After You Read

Check Your Predictions

How close were your predictions to what happened in the story?

My predictions were _____ _____ _____ .

not too close   close   right on

The story is about _____

_____

_____

I _____ the story because _____

(enjoyed / did not enjoy)

Confirm predictions

Reading Focus

*predictions - confirm
judgements*

Writing Focus

summary

Teaching Suggestions

This response activity is an optional follow-up to
the previewing and predicting activity on page
83.

Ask students to think about how accurate their
predictions were and consider why they were
close or not. Remind students that there are no
wrong predictions, so it's okay not to have a
match between the story and one's predictions.

Model how to briefly tell what a story is about by
stating the story problem and solution.

ESL students: Depending on the students'
English proficiency, allow them to demonstrate
understanding in ways other than writing a summary. For example, have them act out what
happened or draw pictures.

Oral Language Activity

Ask students to discuss what, if anything, in the
story surprised them.

Extension Activity

Science / Social Studies / Health
Have students use this response activity as a
follow-up to the predicting activity on page 83.
They will confirm the predictions they made
about the content of their textbook.

Name _____

Dear Journal

Pretend to be a character in the story. Write an entry in your journal for one day in the story. Tell what happened and how you felt about it.

Date _____

This journal belongs to _____

Today, _____

_____

_____

When this happened, I felt _____

_____

Write a journal entry

Reading Focus   *conclusions - character feelings*

Writing Focus   *personal narrative*
                                     point of view

Teaching Suggestions
Remind students to put themselves in the place of the character as they write their journal entries. They should think like the character and use "I."

ESL students: Depending on students' English proficiency, allow them to demonstrate understanding in other ways, i.e., pantomime, using manipulatives, or drawing pictures.

Oral Language Activity
Have students read aloud their journal entries. Before reading aloud, allow students time to rehearse with a partner.

Extension Activity

Writing
Have students do the journal-writing activity for a day at the beginning of the story and a day at the end of the story. Then have them discuss how the character changed from the beginning to the end of the story.

What Do You Think?

Complete the map to tell what you thought about the story.

Story Title

What I liked about the story

What I didn't like about the story

Give the story an overall rating. Color one oval.

(terrible)   (fair)   (good)   (great)   (excellent)

89

Evaluate a story

Reading Focus *judgements*

Writing Focus *opinions*

Teaching Suggestions

Encourage students to support their opinions with specific examples from the selection.

ESL students: Depending on students' stage of English development, you may wish to have limited English proficient students draw pictures to illustrate what they liked or disliked about the story.

Oral Language Activity

Have students share their opinions in small group discussions.

Extension Activity

Social Studies / Science
Have students use the activity to rate a unit they have been studying in social studies or science.

Name

Rate the Story

Complete the sentences to tell what you thought about the story.

1. What did you think about the story? Rate the story on a scale of 1 to 10. Color the **Story Meter** to show your rating.

STORY METER

FANTASTIC!

10
9
8
7
6
5
4
3
2
1

BORING

2. The story was _____

      easy to read   just right   hard to read

3. Two words to describe the story are _____

and _____

4. The part of the story I liked best was _____

This was my favorite part because _____

Reading Focus   *judgements*

Writing Focus   *sentences*
                                     support opinions

Teaching Suggestions
Explain how to rate the story on a scale from 1 to 10 and then demonstrate how to show ratings on the Story Meter.

Brainstorm words that students might use in question 3 to describe their stories. List words on the chalkboard.

ESL students: Help students understand the meanings of the words on the chalkboard by providing examples and pictures or by pantomiming the word's meaning.

Oral Language Activity
Have students pretend to be television book critics and give reviews of the story they read. Explain that in their reviews, students will tell what they thought about the story and support their opinions. Suggest that they use the response activity questions and answers as a basis for their reviews.

Extension Activity

Social Studies / Science
Have students use the response activity to evaluate their social studies or science textbooks.

Name _____

Picture the Place

Choose your favorite part of the story.   Where does it take place?
Write the place in the center of the wheel. Then write the story
words that describe that place. Fill in as many senses as you can.

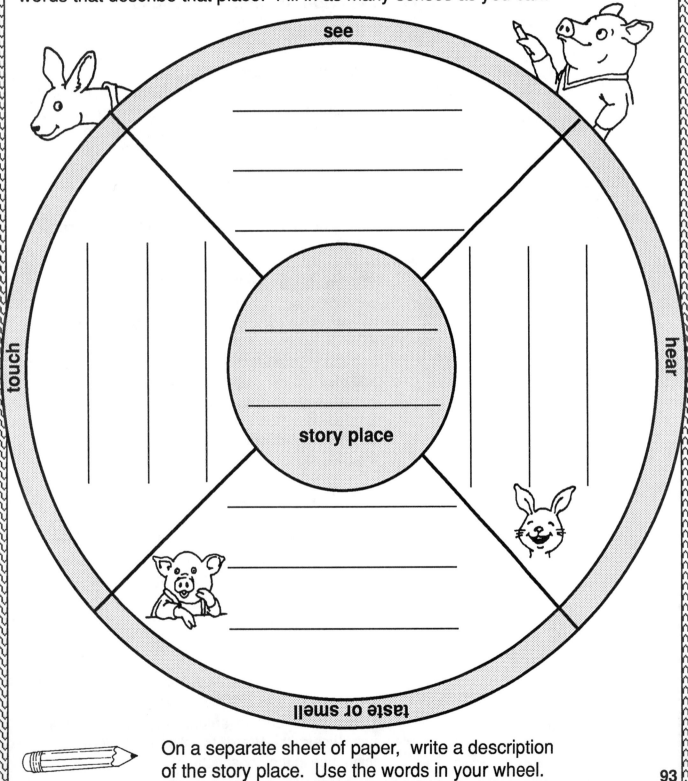

see

touch

hear

story place

taste or smell

On a separate sheet of paper, write a description
of the story place. Use the words in your wheel.

93

Describe setting

Reading Focus

setting

Writing Focus

description - sensory details

Teaching Suggestions

Review setting. Then explain to students that first they should find and list the words the author uses to describe the setting. Then they should imagine the setting and add their own words to further describe it.

You may wish to have some students draw a picture of the setting instead of writing a description of it.

ESL students: Help students understand the concept of *setting* and the words that name the senses. Use examples, pantomime, and pictures.

Pair the ESL student who understands the words and their meanings but is not ready to speak English with an English dominant student. The English dominant student will say a word or a sentence containing a word from the activity, and the ESL student will point to the word.

Oral Language Activity

Have students choose a passage from the story that describes the setting and read it aloud to a small group. Provide time for students to rehearse their passages before reading them aloud.

Extension Activity

Writing

Have students write a description for the setting of an adventure story. After students choose a setting for a good adventure story, direct them to use "Picture the Place" to list sensory words they might use in their descriptions.

Name

Picture It!

Where and when a story takes place is its setting.

Draw a picture to show the story setting.
Then write a title for your picture.

Title: _____

Illustrate the setting

Reading Focus

setting
main idea

Teaching Suggestions

You may want to have students use the activity page to sketch their illustrations and make their final copies on art paper.

ESL students: Help ESL students understand the concept of *setting*. Use examples, pantomime, or pictures.

Oral Language Activity

Have students show their pictures to the class and use descriptive language to describe the setting. As classmates listen, they are to think about what senses the speaker awakens in them. Then have the listeners give feedback to the speaker in which they explain which sensory details were most effective.

Extension Activity

Writing

Have students write a paragraph to describe the setting in their pictures. Encourage students to use descriptive words and phrases that tell what they would see, hear, taste, smell, and feel if they were sitting in the picture

Name _____

What Do You See and Hear?

The setting of a story tells where and when the story takes place. The author helps you picture the story setting by describing its sights and sounds. Fill in the chart with story words that help you see and hear the setting.

STORY SETTING

WHEN   WHERE

SETTING   Where _____

When _____

What do you see?	What do you hear?
1 _____	1 _____
2 _____	2 _____
3 _____	3 _____
4 _____	4 _____

Now think of your own words that could also describe the story setting. Write two words for **See** and **Hear**.

SEE 👀   HEAR

1 _____   1 _____

2 _____   2 _____

Complete a chart

Reading Focus   *setting*

Writing Focus   *description - sensory words*

Teaching Suggestions
Review the concept of *setting*. Have students brainstorm words that describe sights and sounds and record them. Then have students complete the activity.

ESL students: Pair the ESL students who understand the meanings of the words but are not ready to speak with English dominant students. The English dominant students will say words from the board and the ESL students will point to them. Then have pairs work together to complete the activity.

Oral Language Activity
Have students work in pairs to use the words on their charts in sentences.

Extension Activity

Writing
Have students use the words on their charts to write a paragraph that describes the story setting. Encourage students to include their own descriptive words to draw a vivid word picture.

Name

Words! Words! Words!

In each balloon, write a new word from the story.

Choose one word from the balloons. Draw a picture to show the meaning of the word.

Illustrate word meaning

Reading Focus   *find and define new words*

Teaching Suggestions

You may wish to have students work in **cooperative groups** of three to do the activity. First the group will find new words to write in the balloons. Then each group member will illustrate a different word.

ESL students: Have ESL students who understand the meanings of words but are hesitant to speak English work in **cooperative groups** with English dominant students. All group members will display their pictures. Group members will take turns saying a word and using it in a sentence, and the ESL student will locate the word. An English speaker will say the word again, and the ESL students will repeat it.

Oral Language Activity

Have students make up and tell a very short story that illustrates the meaning of one of the words they listed on their papers.

Extension Activity

Social Studies / Science

Have students use the response activity to find and illustrate new words from their science or social studies textbooks.

Name

A Word to the Wise

Choose one new word from the story.
Complete the map to tell about the word.

Word

Word that means the same or almost the same

Picture that shows what the word means

Sentence that uses the word

_____

_____

© Spring Street Press

Complete a word map

Reading Focus   *define and use new words*

Writing Focus   *sentences*

Teaching Suggestions

Explain the concept of synonyms and help students find synonyms for their vocabulary words. Be sure students understand that their sentences should show that they understand the meaning of the new vocabulary word.

ESL students: Have students who speak the same native language work in pairs to do this activity. Allow ESL students to indicate understanding of the vocabulary word by writing their sentences in their native language.

Oral Language Activity

Have students make up and tell a very short story that explains the meaning of their word.

Extension Activity

Creative Dramatics

Have students work in groups to play Charades. Begin by listing the new words students chose from the story. Then have each group choose one word to act out for the rest of the class to guess.

Name

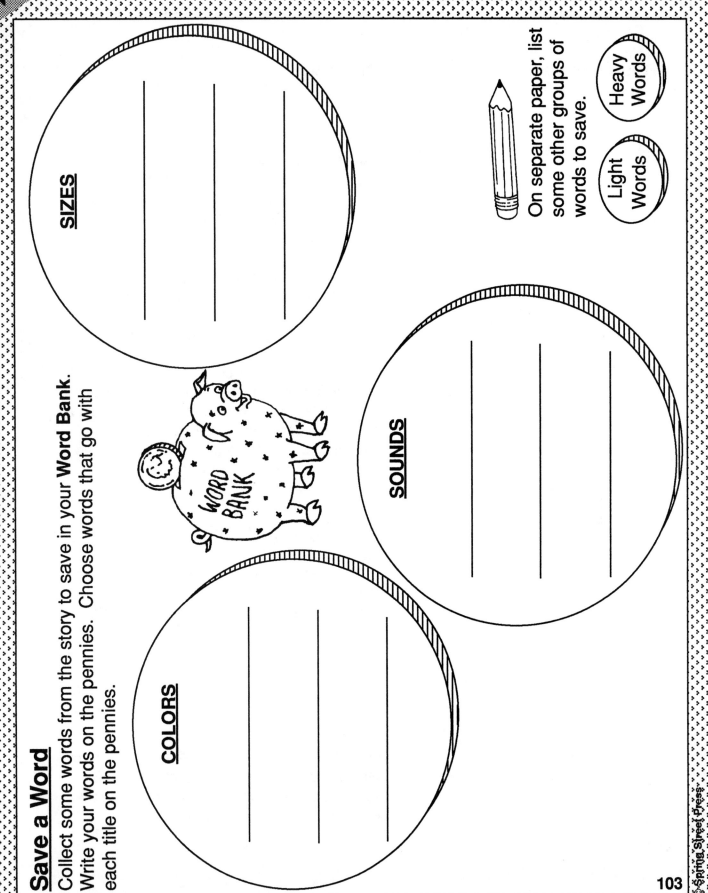

Save a Word

Collect some words from the story to save in your **Word Bank**. Write your words on the pennies. Choose words that go with each title on the pennies.

SIZES

SOUNDS

COLORS

WORD BANK

On separate paper, list some other groups of words to save.

Heavy Words

Light Words

103

List and categorize words

Reading Focus

categorize

Teaching Suggestions

Before students begin, have them brainstorm words that fall into the categories on the activity sheet: colors, sizes, and sounds. Then have them find words in the story.

You may want to extend the activity and have students find and categorize other words from the story, i.e., sensory words; heavy and light words; describing words and action words.

ESL students: For students who understand the meanings of the words but are not ready to speak English, display pictures of words from a category students are studying. Have ESL students locate words after a partner says the word and a sentence containing the word.

Oral Language Activity

Have students use the words in their Word Banks in sentences that show they understand the meanings. Have each student choose a word from the activity page and say a sentence containing the word.

Extension Activity

Science

Have students find and categorize words from their science books. For example, students might find and categorize words related to the seasons: winter, spring, summer, fall.

Name

What's in a Word?

Choose two new words from the story. Then fill in the chart. Write a meaning and personal clue for each word. Or draw pictures to show the meanings and clues.

NEW WORD	WORD MEANING	PERSONAL CLUE TO HELP REMEMBER THE MEANING

NEW!

Complete a word chart

Reading Focus

define new words
relate meaning to personal experience

Teaching Suggestions

Explain that a personal clue is something from the student's own life that he or she associates with the word. For example, a personal clue for *murky* might be the water in a huge mud puddle that forms in the child's backyard. Discuss how personal clues help a person remember a word by linking its meaning to something that the person already knows.

ESL students: Have students with limited English proficiency draw rather than write the word meanings and personal clues.

Encourage ESL students to derive personal clues unique to their culture and then share that aspect of their culture with the class.

Oral Language Activity

Ask students to select one of their words, tell its meaning, and explain their personal clue.

Extension Activity

Social Studies

Have students complete "What's in a Word" for two words from their social studies unit.

Name

What Do You Know? (part 1)

BEFORE YOU READ

Preview
- Look through the selection to find out what it is about.
- Read titles and words in bold print.
- Look at the pictures.
- What is the book about? Write the topic below.

Think Back
- Think about what you already know about the topic.
- On the lines below, make a list of facts you know. Use the back of the page if you need more space.

List

What I already know about _____
(topic)

I know that _____

_____

I know that _____

_____

I know that _____

_____

READ   As you read, look for new information about the topic.

Brainstorm and list

Reading Focus

preview
activate prior knowledge

Writing Focus

list

Teaching Suggestions

You may use this prereading activity alone or in conjunction with the postreading activity on page 109.

Remind students that a selection topic describes what the selection is generally about and is stated in one or two words.

After students complete the activity, have them share the facts they know about the topic with the class and record them on butcher paper. Then have students work in **cooperative groups** to generate questions they have about the topic and hope are answered in the text. Have each group share its questions with the class and record them on a second sheet of butcher paper. Then tell students to read to answer their questions and find new information about the topic.

ESL Students: Have ESL students brainstorm their prior knowledge and generate questions in both languages, especially in their native language. Then have them discuss their ideas in groups with English dominant students.

Oral Language Activity

Have students take turns telling one fact they already know about the topic or one question they have.

Extension

Science / Social Studies

Have students do this response activity before reading their textbooks.

What Do You Know? (part 2)

AFTER YOU READ

What did you learn about the topic?
On the note page below, list new facts you learned.
Use the back of the page if you need more space.

<u>What I Learned</u>

about _____

(topic)

① _____

_____

② _____

_____

③ _____

_____

④ _____

_____

List new learning

Reading Focus

evaluate understanding
integrate new learning

Writing Focus

list

Teaching Suggestions
This postreading activity may be used alone or as a follow-up to the prereading activity on page 107.

Have students share the new information they learned. If you listed questions students had before reading, have them check to see which ones were answered. Then have students suggest questions that they still have about the topic. Discuss where students might find the answers to their questions.

ESL Students: Depending on students' English proficiency, allow ESL students to demonstrate understanding in ways other than writing, i.e., drawing pictures or acting out new learning.

Oral Language Activity
Have students find a paragraph in their text that contains a new fact they learned and read it aloud to a small group. To ensure fluency and proper intonation, allow students time to rehearse before reading aloud to their groups.

Extension

Social Studies / Science
Have students do this postreading activity after reading a chapter or section in their textbooks.

Name _____

Question It

BEFORE
YOU
READ

Preview

Look through the selection.
- Read the titles and words in bold print.
- Look at the pictures

Predict

What is the selection about? _____
                                                    (topic)

What questions do you have about the topic?   Write two questions.

1 _____
_____

?

2 _____
_____

?

READ   Read the selection. Look for
            the answers to your questions.

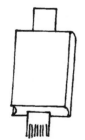

AFTER   Answer your questions. Write your
YOU   answers on separate paper. Or tell
READ   your answers to a classmate.

Write questions

Reading Focus
preview and predict
integrate new learning

Writing Focus
questions and answers

Teaching Suggestions
Review how to preview a text. Remind students that the topic describes what the selection is generally about and is stated in one or two words.

Have individuals share their questions with the class and record them on the chalkboard. Remind students that as they read, they should look for the answers to their questions. Explain that some questions may not be answered. After students answer their questions, discuss which ones were not answered and ask students to suggest where they might find the answers to these questions.

ESL Students: Help students understand the concepts of *previewing* and *predicting*. Use alternate wording such as "looking through," "thinking about ahead of time," "making a good guess" and then model the procedures using familiar books or pictures.

Oral Language Activity
Have students read their questions aloud before they begin reading.

Extension

Research Skills
Have students suggest questions that were not answered in the text. Discuss references students might use to locate the answers to their questions and review how to use them. Then have students work in **cooperative groups** to research and answer one question.

Name _____

Think Ahead - Think Back (part 1)

BEFORE
YOU
READ

Preview
Look through the selection.
- Read titles and words in bold print.
- Look at the pictures.

Predict
What will the selection be about?
Complete the sentences to make your predictions.

I think the selection will be about _____.

(topic)

One idea that I think the author will tell about is _____

_____

_____

Another idea is _____

_____.

I probably will _____ this selection because _____

(enjoy / not enjoy)

_____

_____.

READ   Read the selection. See how close your predictions are.

Complete paragraph frames

Reading Focus *predictions*
previewing

Writing Focus *paragraph frames*

Teaching Suggestions
You may use this prereading activity alone or in conjunction with the postreading activity on page 115.

Review with students how to preview a selection, determine its topic, and make predictions.

ESL Students: Pair ESL students with classmates who speak the students' native language. Have them work on the prediction activity together.

Oral Language Activity
Have students read their predictions aloud.

Extension

Science / Social Studies
Have students use the response activity to make predictions before reading a section or chapter of their textbooks.

Name _____

Think Ahead - Think Back (part 2)

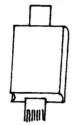

AFTER YOU READ

Complete the paragraph frames to tell what the selection is about.

The selection is about _____.

One important idea that the author tells about is _____

_____

_____.

Another important idea is _____

_____.

I _____ enjoy this selection because _____
         did / did not

_____

_____.

Before you read the selection, you made some predictions about it.
How close were your predictions? Circle one.

      way off   fairly close   right on

Complete paragraph frames

Reading Focus

summarize
reflect on what was read

Writing Focus

paragraph frames

Teaching Suggestions

This postreading activity is designed to be used alone or as a follow-up to the prereading activity on page 113. If you choose to use the activity alone, have students skip the last question.

ESL Students: Allow ESL students to use pictures to indicate their understanding of the selection.

Oral Language Activity

Have students read aloud their completed paragraph frames.

Extension

Science / Social Studies

Have students use the response activity after reading a section or chapter in their textbooks.

BOOKS I HAVE READ

Name

DATE	BOOK TITLE	RATING (1-10)

Name _____

Book Notes

Famous
Duck
Stories

Date _____

    I read _____

by _____ .

    The book is about _____

_____

_____

_____

_____

_____ .

    The best part of the book is _____

_____

_____

_____ .

Name

Reading I Do at Home

Date	Book Title	Minutes Read	Parent's Initials

Name

Daily Reading File

Date _____ Pages Read Today _____

Title _____

Tell what happened in the part of the story you read today.

_____

_____

_____

_____

Date _____ Pages Read Today _____

Title _____

Tell what happened in the part of the story you read today.

_____

_____

_____

_____

Daily Reading Log

Name _____

Date	Book Title	Pages Read Today

Name

Today I Read ...

Date _____   How many pages did you read today? _____

Title _____

**Draw a picture to show what happened
in the part of the story you read today.**

Date _____   How many pages did you read today? _____

Title _____

**Draw a picture to show what happened
in the part of the story you read today.**

Name

For the Week of

Weekly Reading Chart

TOTAL PAGES READ THIS WEEK

Monday

TITLE

NUMBER OF PAGES I READ

Tuseday

TITLE

NUMBER OF PAGES I READ

Wednesday

TITLE

NUMBER OF PAGES I READ

Thursday

TITLE

NUMBER OF PAGES I READ

Friday

TITLE

NUMBER OF PAGES I READ

Name _____

Daily Reading Journal

Date _____   I read _____ pages today.

My book is _____.

I _____ what I read today because
            enjoyed / did not enjoy

_____

_____

_____

_____ .

Date _____   I read _____ pages today.

My book is _____.

I _____ what I read today because
            enjoyed / did not enjoy

_____

_____

_____ .

ALSO AVAILABLE FROM SPRING STREET PRESS ...

Responding to Literature Grades 1-3

- 58 creative Response Activities
- 8 Record-Keeping Charts
- teaching ideas for ESL students
- suggestions for developing oral language skills

.....................................$15.95

Responding to Literature: Writing and Thinking Activities

- • contains generic activities that go with <u>any</u> selection
- • integrates reading and writing
- • promotes creative and critical thinking
- • extends reading beyond the selection

Each book is packed with fully reproducible reading Response Activities that can be used with any reading selection and Record-Keeping Charts to assist you in monitoring and managing students' reading. The Response Activities may be used in a variety of ways to adapt to your reading curriculum and teaching style as well as to the varied abilities and learning styles of your students.

Typical response activities include writing in all forms – narrative, descriptive persuasive and expository – and in a variety of modes – poems, letters, short stories, news stories, journal entries and many, many more. Motivating and imaginative activities such as creating advertisements, book jackets, coats of arms, and tee shirt slogans capture students' attention and hold their interest.

Responding to Literature Grades 4-8

- 75 open-ended Response Activities
- 8 Record-Keeping Charts

....$15.95

AVAILABLE IN SPANISH
Motivando La Lectura
Actividades de Razonamiento en Torno a la Literatura

Motivando la Lectura Grados 1-3
........................$16.95

Motivando la Lectura Grados 4-8
..........................$16.95

HELP STUDENTS BECOME STRATEGIC READERS AND LEARNERS

Strategies for Reading Nonfiction
Comprehension and Study Activities
Grades 4-8

- • contains over 40 reproducible Comprehension and Study Activities plus 10 Strategy Guides

- • may be used with any nonfiction selection
  - textbooks
  - trade books
  - articles and essays

- • provides a variety of activities that help students read, understand and learn from expository text

....$15.95

Prereading and follow-up postreading activities develop strategic readers.

Guided reading strategies help students monitor their comprehension and think as they read.

Study and writing activities help students read for main ideas, summarize, and write expository paragraphs.

Strategy Guides help students apply key reading-study skills including setting purpose for reading, previewing and predicting, and taking notes.

ORDER FORM

Name _____

Shipping Address _____

_____

City _____ **State** _____ **Zip** _____

Qty.	Title	Price	Amt.
	Responding to Literature gr. 1-3	$15.95	$
	Responding to Literature gr. 4-8	$15.95	$
	Strategies / Nonfiction gr. 4-8	$15.95	$
	Motivando La Lectura gr. 1-3	$16.95	$
	Motivando La Lectura gr. 4-8	$16.95	$
	Shipping & Handling (see chart for amt.)		$
	TOTAL ENCLOSED (All payments must be in US Funds.)		$

Shipping Charges	in US	to Canada
1 book	4.00	4.50
2 books	4.50	5.00
3-5 books	5.50	6.00
6-9 books	7.25	11.00
10-15 books	11.00	14.00

**Mail orders with payment to
Spring Street Press
2606 Spring Blvd.
Eugene, OR 97403**

Payment Method:

☐ Check ☐ VISA/Mastercard

Credit Card Number _____ **Expiration Date** _____

Signature _____
(Credit card charges must have signature.)